AF508809

First Publication Date: Sep 2019
ISBN: 978-81-939295-6-8
₹300 | US $9.99| £7.99
Originally Published in Paperback
Cover Photograph: Azif Mohammad Iqbal
Cover Design: Linda Ashok

Manufactured in India, published & funded
by RLFPA Editions (OPC) Pvt Ltd.

'En' is a unit of measurement half of an 'em' dash. In a patriarchal society, a woman is always considered half of a man. EN BODY breaks the convention to establish new literary authority and aesthetics.

EN BODY

CONTENTS

Poems by

MEERA NAIR

meeramyworld.com
meeranairarun@gmail.com

DEPARTURE LOUNGE

The woman at the counter –
lipstick, the color of blood
skin, the color of honey –
pries open my baggage

'It's only words,' I say
A whirlpool of thoughts,
incessant words:
dark
dense
raw.
Stripped bare

She pastes a piece of paper on it
'It's heavy,' she says.
The label says 'fragile.'

My baggage
proud and fragile
travels alone on a pulsating
metallic belt.

Heavy; because he had never cared.

KONARK

Where your heart once was
now lies a hollow.
Did it hurt when they took it away?
Was sand all you could find to fill the void?

The salt of the sea eats into you
There are pockmarks on your face
Does it sting when it rains?

Your lions roar no more
Your horses have broken their backs
Your lotuses are half-eaten
A salamander runs over your body
It sticks out its tongue
Snakes live in your crevices

Your women have lost their breasts
Your men their libido
Your wheels crumble
The chariot does not move

Plundered
Looted
Eroded
Falling
How long will the scaffolding hold?

And yet,
I fall on my knees to worship you.

For even in your ruins
There is so much glory

WOMEN ON THE STREETS

All I take is a look
to pack them swiftly into little boxes,
neatly labeled.

On the top,
light and languid –
the ones who live in the bliss
of ignorance.

In the middle, those who bear
it well with coats of paint
and designer blouses.

At the bottom is the precious
lot, staggering
under the weight
of choices made.
I watch these women on the streets.

DELUGE*

The last of our stories have run dry.

Noah's Ark lies deserted,
church walls have given away.
The only God
the only Truth
is elsewhere.

The bachelor boy perches
atop his mountain
among the plethora of Gods,
of a million colors and a million shapes,
who have all drowned?

The goats have all been slaughtered.
From the minarets
arise the sounds of silence

The atheist's notebook lies empty
for the Gods are all dead.

Yet we live.

From Water we came
to Water, we will return.

DENTIST

The dentist lays out the tools of his trade:
scalpel, saw, scissors, spade,
all gleaming bright.

Freshly sterilized, he says with a flourish.

A single prick of a needle
and I go numb.
Maybe this is what it is to be you:
sans desire

The dentist heaves, shoves, and pulls.
Encased in a cotton wad
he hands me my tooth.

I refuse to open my eyes.

Later, a little later
it bleeds.

No, I am not you

There is a gaping wound
and throbbing pain;
it hurts.
Later, much later
the dentist cuts away a piece of thread.
He says I have healed.

But at night
your absence fills my mouth.

My tongue continues to seek you.

EMOTICONS

Emoticons changed the world.

You sent me a heart-shaped red;
it throbbed on my screen
and I was afraid the glass would crack.

I hated the thumbs-up sign
so you replaced it with sunglasses on a face.

You blew flying kisses,
stuck out your tongue,
folded your hands,
and sent me your lips.

Then there was a yellow face
with hands sticking out of its sides –
you told me it was a hug.

I should have sent a smiley in return
Instead, I switched off my phone.

Sometimes I wonder what your touch feels like.

BISON

The first time I saw him
he had come to quench his thirst
at a water hole.
He drank like a thief –
sly, greedy
and in haste.

I traced the contours of his hoof prints
I breathed the air that his flapping tail stirred up
I stalked his prey.

Then I fed on him from near
I touched his sleek hide
and dangled from the horns on his head.

Have you ever seen a wild bison
that you have wanted?
To tame.
To own.
To possess.

CIRCUS

The tent
is a piece of the sky.
A slice of rainbow cake.
'One Ms. Neha from Nepal'
announces the microphone,
she appears in shimmering red:
fair, slender and expressionless,
the trapeze act begins
she flings herself from bar to bar
swings, flies
twists, turns,
head over heels,
sometimes she freezes mid-way.
Far below
a frayed net
awaits a fall.
The clown is in tattered clothes
he has run out of jokes
and drinks endless buckets of water,
a flapping fish
perpetually caught between his lips.
The fire eater
chews his share of fire,
swallows the flames
and hides the rest inside his pants.
The many Nehas

Raise their legs
And rotate their heads.
beads of sweat glisten
on their flat, bared bellies.
A hundred kitchen plates
come flying on his face;
he smiles all through the balancing act.
The juggler, strangely, is not a woman.
A motley crowd of Africans
hip hop to the beats of a tribal song:
they flip,
somersault,
alight poles
and walk on their hands,
their rippling muscles throbbing with life.
A starving horse
gallops in circles.
With mouths bandaged
camels walk the ramp.
Dogs dance
and parrots say Namaste.
The motorcyclist
dons his helmet and gloves
and rides his bike in dizzying circles
inside the well of death.
The ringmaster is
omniscient,
omnipresent,
omnipotent.;
maybe
he works according to a plan.

FOR TENZIN TSUNDUE *

We sit across each other –
a study in contrasts,
his nose flat as the Tibetan plateau
mine a Western Ghat peak.

The red bandana on his forehead
flutters in the evening breeze,
The orange bindi on mine
does not budge an inch.

When he smiles
his face disappears into wrinkles,
when I do
my mouth eats my face.

He owns two black shirts,
my wardrobe is a riot of colors;
the soles of his shoes are worn out
my car keys jingle.

He wakes up in a new city
each day,
I live and die in the same city
everyday.

We sit across each other –
a study in contrasts,
yet we both know
that we both speak the same language

that of the homeless.

Tenzin Tsundue is a Tibetan activist and poet

KOLKATA

Kolkata you boast of history;
the Ganges flows,
you reek of poverty…

Horses trot
around your guarded memorials,
pulling along gaudy carriages
in your alleys.
Men trot
carrying the burden of other men
on their shoulders.

The red of the pan that stains your mouth
and the white of your rosogollas
color the saris
that hang out of the windows
of your dilapidated buildings.

A lone tram
trudges its way through streets
teeming with people.

Kolkata,
your Goddess sticks out her tongue
at your children
begging on your streets.

GREAT GRANDMOTHER

My great grandmother
refused to comb her hair.

Her curls grew into tangles,
the tangles into knots
and birds built their nests
on her head.

The tiles on the roof cracked,
the kitchen caved in first.
Weeds spread their slender arms on window panes,
the deer horns in the drawing-room splintered

The well outside dried up and
the house fell.
But the roses in the courtyard
bloomed wild!

My great grandmother
lay on her cot

day and night.
She did not keep count of her children –
some became widows,
some died.

My great grandmother
lay on her cot
on a hundred fluffy pillows as
her skin grew pink and
her teeth black.
She did not budge an inch.

From my great grandmother
I inherited the color of my skin,
these curls on my head
and a hundred fluffy pillows.

But sadly
not her great
Art of supreme Detachment

JESUS, DIE

Die, die, die
Each time you leave
I will you to die.

No goblet of wine,
no food-laden table
but so many last suppers on the same plate.
I betrayed you thirty times.

Die, die, die.

But each time
you return from your cave
I take a look at the look on your face,
of being perpetually nailed to the cross,
and I bleed.

There is so much hopelessness
in your resurrection,
I think we got the stories mixed up.

Maybe it is I
who must die.

LAMENTS OF A RELUCTANT FEMINIST

For the man who believes
his worth lies in the piece of flesh
between his legs,
you feel a near maternal love
for you have seen him melt at your breasts.

The man who brandishes swords and guns
has not known the red of menstrual blood,
you forgive him his ignorance.

The man who flaunts his brute strength
comes in handy;
he can carry the heaviest piece of luggage.

The man who swears and curses,
calls others motherfuckers
and drowns bottles
will never know what it is like
when a baby latches on to your nipples.

Men are such ignorant darlings
It is so difficult being a feminist

YOU

your presence
your absence
your absent presence

there is no word for this
this Love
this Longing
this Emptiness
this Despair

there is no word for this
only this constant ache

even in not wanting you
there is this you
that I cannot escape

RENTED QUARTERS

The old man turns up without fail
Every month

There is a locked-up room here
That he cannot let go of

Last night
My knee brushed against a secret drawer
Hidden beneath the dining table
Inside was a treasure trove
Buttons of different colors
A needle pierced into a spool of thread
A book of poems
And a half-empty box of vermillion

Though I light no lamp
I keep the beaded curtain covering the prayer room
Polished and bright

I live in a house
Someone else has loved in

THE LORD FALLS ILL

On a full moon night
he fell ill.
The sick room is dark,
his ever rages,
his body is on fire,
he burns.
The temple ground is forlorn,
diyas flutter
and die in the evening breeze.
Monkeys huddle together,
mud pots lie empty of Mahaprasad
even the flies lose their buzz.
Raj Vaidya brings him medicines,
devotees fruits and cheese;
they offer him oil and musk,
water and fresh paint.
He refuses.
But when the fever rages
his body burns hot
and he is not himself.
The Lord becomes human,
he asks for me.
It is then that He wants me.

PS: On the day of Jyestha Purnima, Dev Snana is performed. Lord Jagannath is made to have a bath with 108 vessels of water from a specific well. Right after the shower, Lord Jagannath falls ill with a fever. He stays away from the public for 15 days. After this, begins the famous Rath Yathra.

THIRUVANANTHAPURAM

You ask, what difference does it make
whether we are in the same city?

The sedate white columns of the Secretariat blush,
they turn red and pink,
the Padmatheertham brims, it overflows.
Christ atop Palayam Palli
opens his arms wider,
his golden glow fills the night.
Vayalar's bust at Vellayambalam
hums a love song
on the Museum grounds.
The old and young
hold hands,
the clock atop University building stands still.
Trains do a jig at Thambanoor station,
Pangode military station lays down its arms,
the concrete monstrosity jutting out
into Kowdiar junction
retreats with grace.
Animals roam free in the zoo,
the stone mermaid at Shanghumugham
Goes for a dip in the sea

I could cross this Mathrubhumi road
and run into you

if we are in the same city.

ARTIST

The artist picks up a brush,
steals the pink of the evening sky
& mixes it with the red of his blood;
a painting is born.
There are listless words;
lonely and lost
that float in the air
and fill the writer's pen.
A streak of lightning
illuminates the sky,
& a golden crab scuttles back home.
The evening breeze
embraces the shore.
Somewhere, a star is born.
The Gods must be in so much pain.

ATTUKAL PONGALA*

Her smile is a perfect curve
sans a crease,
her cotton sari
pinned and pleated.

They bring pots and bricks,
some small eats,

they fill her room
with small talk and smoke.

What she gives away
comes back,
containers overflow
Pongala Payasam will find its way
to some garbage heap.

My city has played the perfect hostess
and now that the guests have left
she will wash the dirty plates.

*Atukal Pongala is a religious festival celebrated in Trivandrum

BALANCE SHEET

I learned them by heart
the golden rules of debit and credit,

it is with the ruthlessness of a seasoned clerk
that I draw up accounts.

Boredom on the left,
imagination on the right,
honesty, impatience,
love, narcissism,
compassion, curiosity,
broken hearts on either side.
All measured,
weighed,
neatly classified.

But defying labels
it hangs in mid-air,
it sticks out like my second toe
longer than my big toe
this 'the inability to toe the line.'

My balance sheet
does not balance.

THE BOOK OF POEMS

Do you know what it is like
to make a book out of my poems?
Like a voyeur,
I stare at my own words,
& I cringe at every line.
I watch my own words from afar
and wonder who wrote them?
Then I read your invisible lines,
smile,
and gather my poems in my arms.
I leave the first-page blank
because I cannot write your name.
But before I close this book,
there is the last page that I must fill...
On it, I shall write
an ode to your impotence.

BRIDES OF GOD

Sister Betty;
angel's face
& devil's heart,
locked up the throw-ball
every break.
Once she opened a cupboard
to take out the Bible
and was horrified to find that
someone had stored there a packet of
sanitary pads!

Sister Rasna
lorded the backstage
and served secret helpings
of orange-colored water
to me, the teacher's ever thirsty daughter.

Sister Olive,
plump and fair
who rolled her 'r' s
and believed that perfect English could guarantee
you free passage to Heaven.

I forget their names.
Penguins?
Ridiculous veils,
black and white,
billowing in the wind
as we peeked
to see if underneath hid
long flowing hair
or ugly bald heads.

My mother;
convent educated
& convent employed,
bowed in reverence.
I wondered
if these brides of God
were any happier
than the brides of Men

COMRADE AND I

Comrade and I boarded the last bus,
a waft of breeze from somewhere lent a brief life
to the curls resting on my forehead.
"You are beautiful," he said.
Comrade held forth on bourgeois socialism.
We passed by an animal farm,
he then moved on to relative deprivation.
I polished his silver spoon,
comrade dwelt on the dictatorship of the proletariat –
power oozed from every word.
The sky, he declared, is always a crimson red;
night had begun to put forward its stealthy steps,
and when we got off the bus
He said,
"Love is a luxury that must be rationed."

DIDI

Didi sprouted in our neighborhood
like a mushroom after the rains.

She came from the mountains
and had lived in the cold
with tigers.
Snakes danced to her tunes,
birds ate from her hands,
and trees blossomed to her wishes.

We too heeded to her call.

The women arrived in various sizes
of bulging bottoms
and thunder thighs.
We inhaled through one nostril
and exhaled through the other
eager for a magic cure
for our lost bodies
and broken minds.

Communal Payasam served in generous helpings,
we lapped it up
hardly smelling the 'Tva' in disguise.

Soon it became the opium of the masses.

Didi stood on one leg,
stuck out her tongue,
and panted like a dog.
She rolled backwards,
sat like a lotus,
and lay down like the dead.

'Stretch, stretch,'
she commanded the crowd,
and to the gasping me she said
'Close your mouth and learn to enjoy the pain.'

DIVINE

There are easy ways –
age-old beliefs
carved on centuries-old stone,
generations of faith
fed on prescription pills of truth,
incessant chanting
fire, oil and lit lamps,
routine and rhythm:
saviors.
And retreat
but to love you
to love the flawed you
to love the deaf, dumb, blind you
without being loved in return
is so much more divine.

DOG

Silence seeps into my ears
and plays a nonstop track
that cannot be turned off.
Emptiness is tangible,
it is weighed
and strapped to my chest.

Each time the phone beeps,
like Pavlov's dog,
I salivate

DRUNK

Tonight I am too tired
to empty half your vodka bottle
in the sink
and replace it with water:
my prayer for your liver to live a little longer.

What is it that the night
does to me,
that I can longer
pretend to be sober?

Drunk on love
tonight once again
I must pick up a pen
and turn despair
into words on paper.

IDOLS SHATTER

A slap across the face:
blinding,
a snake bite
stinging,
a jet of boiling water
scalding,
A blow on the skull,
cracking.
Lorry wheels on the body,
crushing.
When idols shatter
They do so in one go
It is only after a while
That pain begins its endless flow

IT MUST END

No, you are not a fingertip away
like an unborn child
that haunts my womb;
I carry you
in me.

Closure:
as evasive as the last word
as fresh as the last wound
leers at me.

I dream all-day
I dream all night
of dying
in your arms.

KATHUA

I do not speak of
green meadows,
or galloping horses,
or rag dolls,
or venom spewing Gods.

Instead, I tell my husband,
I am glad we have sons
and not daughters.

KOVALAM

A perfect curve:
sun-kissed
wave licked
embraced by sand.
The lighthouse in striped pajamas
stands tall.
During the day, crowds trample its insides,
at night
it throws everyone out
and basks in the glory of its light.
A woman holds her man
she wills the world to watch,
dogs mate on the sand,
bodies of all shapes and colors,
and the salt of the sea.
Lobster, squid, and crab on ice,
their mouths and eyes wide open,
a large fish caught in surprise.
Lamp posts,
a paved walkway,
and an empty police aid post.
Tibetan lizards,
Kashmiri pashminas,
Rajasthani wrap-around.
Ripe mangoes,
silver, jade, and seashell,
Krishna, Siva, and Che Guevara tattooed tees,
catamarans on land
pining for the sea.
Many a time
one is a tourist
in one's land.

LAST LOVE

If you are a man's last love,
do not fret
that it is too late.
Men are slow.
The grey on their temples should show,
wrinkles must encase his eyes,
he must know what it is to lose for sure;
there must be scars on his arm
that you can run your fingers across
till he says, it hurts no more.
If you are a man's last love
count yourself fortunate
for only by then
would he have learned
to love.

MY LOVE IS A TERRIBLE THING

My love is a terrible thing
I know what it does to you.

It makes you swim for hours
in the depths of your green pond.

It makes you take long walks
along the coastline
with your children,
their fingers intertwined in yours.

It makes you take your hands off
the steering wheel
and let your car drive into
a parked lorry
on a deserted street
on a lonely night.

My love is a terrible thing.

NERO

Nero, there you stand
atop your hill palace
strumming your lyre,

the city burns
the wind is wild
flames leap from alley to alley.

Look at the trail of destruction you set off:
broken homes,
broken hearts.

When the fire dies
you will build your golden palace
on these charred grounds.

But Nero, do not stop singing
for I move to the rhythm of the notes
that escape your lips.

Nero, the city burns –
come, watch me dance.

NO MORE ONAM

His foot on my head.

How much does one shrink in the name of love?
Where does it blur,
the razor-thin line between ego and self-respect?

How long does one play games
with a man in disguise?

Three cowardly steps
and a consolation prize.

Had I been Mahabali,
I would have thrown
the condescension in his face.

Here in hell
it is dark
but there is no deceit.

OCKHI

The shore holds an ocean of tears,
the howling wind
drowns the cries of women;
The sea flaunts its might,
waves somersault,
a catamaran flips.

Marinated with spices:
a sprinkling of black pepper
a drop of vinegar
and a pinch of salt

on my plate
lies untouched,
a piece of fried fish.

OFFICE CABIN

Glass windows
glass doors
glass ceiling –
a claustrophobic expanse.

Fold your wings,
sink into a revolving chair,
fall in line.

Outside
it rains.

OOTACAMUND

Sleep rolls a blanket
around your tongue,
your words slur,
frost traces patterns
on your cracked lips.

The night's silence
spills over to day.

There are no crevices
on the closed door
in the dark.
How does one read between sentences?

I must learn
not to fill your absence
with words,
I must learn
not to display my silly soul on an empty page
And call it poetry.

I must learn
to let go.

ORCHARD

How you rushed into the peach orchard,
a picking basket in your hand.
Your long legs strode over the fertile earth,
I could barely keep up.

Don't pluck them all; I called out
but you didn't stop to listen.
You were hungry
you reached for them all:
the nimble blossoms
the overripe ones
the ones just right.
You were hungry

How beautiful it was,
your hunger.

Don't bite off more than you can chew, I said
but you paid no heed.
You were greedy.
You ate with relish,
stuffing your mouth
smacking your lips.
You were greedy.

How beautiful it was,
your greed.

Then it rained
and you turned the basket upside down
over your head.

Slowly,
I starve
to death

RAILWAY STATION

The escalator gleams under neon lights.
A one-way ride to the top
if you land on the right step.
For the journey down, you take the steps.
Traveling alone
dragging your baggage behind
as eateries flaunt display boards of rebirth:
today's vada
tomorrow's rasa vada,
yesterday's rice
today's Appam –
The unending cycle of karma.
Hawkers and beggars,
television screens, and mobile phones,
magazines that flutter in the night breeze...
No one reads books.
The waiting rooms smell of pining,
of endless longing,
and the dust of trains that rush past
without stopping.
The railway station longs to shut its eyes
to close its doors
to switch off its lights
but there are always men,
though no one stays,
there are always men who come and go
and the far-away whistle of a train that never arrives.

RANG NIVAS PALACE*

The King brandishes his sword,
he has conquered a massive wall.
There he stands –
a painting larger than life

His tigers stare at him from across the hall
they refuse to shut their mouths,
their teeth decay.

The colors of Rang Nivas palace have faded.

Hunting dogs
have been replaced
by sausage-shaped canines.

Menu cards
have replaced
scrolls of honor.

The clock on the wall
ticks relentlessly,
time refuses to stand still.

The Princess takes orders –
she serves coffee
to weary tourists.

* *Rang Vilas is a palace in Udaipur that now functions as a hotel*

SHARMILA

Sharmila, you come here in search of solitude?
Have all those years of nasal drip
taught you nothing?
Has the number ninety
not taught you anything either?
Sharmila, you must leave for lands
where no one stares,
you must wear what you please,
dance in the rain,
kiss under the open sky,
and loiter on sidewalks all night.
Here they will flash pictures of your skin and bones.
Here they will drag you into their senseless debates.
Here they will mock your Inaphi.
Here they will ask you to oil your curly locks.
Run, Sharmila, run,
feed that rag doll body of yours
till honey no longer tastes bitter on your tongue.
Sharmila, do not come here in search of solitude,
all you will find is loneliness

SWANSONG

I tasted,
bit on,
chewed,
and swallowed
each word you said.

Now they rise like bile
and paint my mouth
a rancid yellow.

Now in the graveyard of your silence
my words are tombstones
sans inscriptions.

I have sung your song
out of tune
a thousand times.

Men leave,
men come back.
But does any man ever stay?

WORLD'S LARGEST GATHERING OF WOMEN*

To drop a handful of rice
into boiling water
in a baked clay pot
and feed on this frenzy of Faith

to jump into this raging inferno,
light a hearth,
scorch my skin,
and burn my flesh

to pray,
promise,
thank,
wish,
barter,
broker deals,
and atone for my sins…

How I wish I could become one
with these women on the streets.

but my madness has always been solitary,
my madness is mine alone.

I cannot join these women on the streets.

*Attukal Pongala is an annual religious festival celebrated in Thirivananthapuram, the capital of Kerala. It is touted as the largest gathering of women in the world.

YOU AND I

I lean over the rusted balcony railings
I could fall off at any moment now.

My entire universe rests in you.

Of all the colors of the sky
I love the crimson best –
an unsure orange,
an unsure pink,
crimson that turns an inky blue
and becomes one with the night.

The sun is a glowing ball of fire.
The fickle moon
some days a silver streak
from my balcony.
I watch the rain clouds gather
and I watch them part.

How endless,
how vast
is the sky,

how insignificant
are you and I.

WITHDRAWAL

Withdrawal
is a throbbing headache,
an incessant pounding against the temples,

withdrawal is craving,
longing,
every cell of the body on fire,

withdrawal
is burning veins,
coagulated blood,

withdrawal is insomnia,
unsteady hands,

withdrawal is muffled cries
caught in a parched throat,

withdrawal is an unbearable thirst…

Does the sea rage,
does it roar
does it go mute?
Does it bleed,
does it die
when it recedes?

TILL DEATH DO US PART

I come back to an empty room:
linen neatly folded,
pillows in place,
not a crease on the bedspread.

An old newspaper
tattered at the ends
lies on the side table,
a used cup rests on it.
The brown stains on its rim
the color of your cigarette stained teeth.

I come back to frayed toothbrushes,
a tongue cleaner that could be yours or mine

The air conditioner perspires in the heat,
beads of sweat drip from its corners;
it continues its steady snoring.

A pair of your dirty socks
hides in the folds of my creased dupatta
lying on the floor
unwashed.
I come back.

Didn't you even realize
that I was gone?

THE SEA

Last night
the air smelled of salt.

Do you know
what it is
to drive through deserted streets
when the city sleeps?

I have become a voyeur of sorts –
lone lamp posts,
drowsy trees,
mating dogs,
broken hearts,
unfinished stories,
painted feet,
lies and deceit.

I let my poetry die –
dressed it up in satin and lace,
and buried it
in deep wounds.

But last night,
the air smelled of salt
and once again
I became the sea.

SHOPPING MALL

Once I flocked to shopping malls,
hopped on to escalators
and lost count of floors.

Mannequins stared into space,
ice creams became softies,
women became brands,
and promotions overtook displays.

Money was plastic,
bowling alleys had shutters;
one could get on a speeding bike
and not move an inch;
cheese popcorn stuck to your tooth
and movie halls had cushions.

Once I flocked to shopping malls
but not any longer
for I have discovered
the raging ocean,
the endless sky,
flowing rivers,
mighty mountains,
wild forests
and flowering trees
in me.

ABSENCE

Dog-like
I follow your trail.

The first time
you smelled of desire –
raw, dark, and dense.

The next time
of pretense –
washed, ironed, and perfumed.

And then of sweat,
salt and musk.

But the strongest smell of all
is that of your absence,
that flows through my nostrils,
chokes my throat,
and fills my chest.

Your smell
has replaced
my breath.

ANONYMITY

Anonymity is a bullet bike
cutting through the throbbing crowd,
the wind blowing in my hair,
my breasts are seeking your warmth.

Anonymity is a cup of coffee –
yours salted,
mine sugared,
bitter-sweet –
that tastes of your tongue

Anonymity is a wrinkled sheet,
rivulets of your sweat
finding a home
in the ocean of my body.

Anonymity is a poem
sans title
sans poet.

Have you kissed someone on the mouth
in a bustling street
under a full moon?

GREY

There is this grey country
beyond the sea
where longing wraps itself
around you and me

I count the strands of grey on your chest;
one for each year
I did not know your touch

The frostbites on my breast
are the shape of your teeth

Sound waves froze in mid-air
Hailstones raining on my ears
Your voice seeks me

Through the swirling mist
I catch a glimpse of your Red

When I bleed
I bleed all alone

My country is White.

HAJI ALI

When the waves receded
there appeared a causeway
A pathway leading to you
Beggars on either side
sans limbs
sans eyes.
Me too seeking alms –
precariously perched on slippery rocks.
Lovers clinging to each other

not knowing what to ask for
I came to pay homage to the dead
to press my forehead against your cold tomb

I flew through a rain-soaked sky
to reach you before sunset
before the Qawwali singers sang their souls out,
before the hungry sea
drew them doomed lovers
into her bosom,
before the rising tide cut you off
from me.

The sea murmurs
too late
too late.

KAMALA

Kamala;
lotus in eternal bloom,

you stole words from my mouth
and made them yours
long before I was born.

As I turn your pages,
we laugh together
at all those
who read us wrong.

SUMMER

Fruits?
Bats?
Inverted nipples?
What are we?

Upside down
from the branches of a lone tree
we hang

The pond below
hasn't dried up yet.
Whispers of water rise;
they become the sweat on our brows

Parched throats
glistening bodies,
this heat
this sickening, oppressive heat
that presses against our eyes,
weighs against our chests,
and sets our entrails burning.
Do we breathe?
We dream
of ice,
snow,
rain.

At night,
we come Alive..

TEA

How desolate your teacups;
tall,
hefty,
empty.

Lay your head against my womb,
drink from my breasts
to your heart's content.

He who made Woman,
made her a perennial river.

Allow me
to make you
a cup of tea.

TINSEL TOWN

He sweeps me off my feet,
places me on the palm of his hand.

He dresses me up
in colors of his choice
and disrobes me at will.

He paints me
in myriad shades,
marvels at my blemish-free skin.

He draws me into his embrace
needy
every night.

He locks me up in his golden caravan,
turns on dazzling lights,
and speeds away to other lands;

heady,
fickle,
cinema.

TO WOMEN WHO HAVE LOVED

How beautiful your trembling lips.
The rose of your cheeks,
your doe eyes brimming with tears.

Plant a tree.
Climb a mountain.
Watch the sunrise.
Dance away to glory.
Write a poem.
Read a book.

Here, precious,
here is a hug.
HEAL.

WATERFALL

Reckless undercurrents;
Beneath, ripple-less calm —
whirlpools
in incessant twirl —
a cascading waterfall
that falls into bottomless depths.

Sorry, I did not mean to drown you
but this is the only way I flow.

WORLD POETRY DAY

How many times
do we seek the hurt
so that words bleed?

How many times
do we go back to wounds
dig deep
refuse to let them heal
so that words take birth?

Poetry is a lonely terrain.

But maybe on this day
we must gather together,
light lamps in the dark,
and let shadows speak.

Maybe on this day at least
we must throw away our pens
give each other roses

and let wounds and words rest.